Addressing Social Issues in India

C. P. Kumar

Reiki Healer & Author

Roorkee - 247667, India

Disclaimer

While every effort has been made to ensure the accuracy and completeness of the content in this book, the author cannot guarantee that the information contained herein is error-free, up-to-date, or suitable for every individual circumstance.

The author shall not be held liable or responsible for any errors or omissions in the content of the book, nor for any damages, or losses that may arise from any actions taken based upon the suggestions or contents presented in the book.

Readers are advised to use their own judgment and discretion in applying the information provided in this book, and to consult with qualified professionals before taking any action based on the contents of this book. The author disclaims any and all liability or responsibility for any actions taken or not taken based on the information contained in this book.

DEDICATION

To the resilient spirit of India,

This book is dedicated to the diverse tapestry of voices that echo across the vast landscape of this nation. It pays homage to the indomitable spirit of individuals, communities, and organizations tirelessly working towards addressing social issues in India. It is a tribute to those who strive for positive change, challenge societal norms, and contribute to the ongoing narrative of progress.

To the unsung heroes on the ground, the activists, the advocates, the educators, and the change-makers who, day by day, weave a narrative of hope and transformation. Your dedication and passion light the way for a better tomorrow.

To the marginalized and the voiceless, whose struggles form the core of the social issues addressed within these pages. May this book amplify your stories, aspirations, and dreams, serving as a beacon of awareness and empathy.

To the policymakers and administrators who play a pivotal role in shaping the destiny of the nation. May this work inspire thoughtful reflection and informed decisions that foster inclusivity, justice, and social well-being.

To the youth, the torchbearers of change, whose energy and commitment propel the nation towards a brighter future. May your activism and idealism lead to lasting societal transformations.

To the artists, writers, and storytellers who capture the nuances of our society, reflecting both its flaws and its beauty. Your creative expressions have the power to inspire collective introspection and action.

May this dedication symbolize a collective call to action, an acknowledgment of the challenges that persist, and a commitment to fostering a socially just, inclusive, and compassionate India. May the words within these chapters contribute to the ongoing dialogue on social issues, and may they inspire meaningful change for generations to come.

With gratitude and hope,

C. P. Kumar

CONTENTS

PREFACE

In the intricate tapestry of India's diverse and dynamic society, a myriad of social challenges weave through the fabric of everyday life. This book, "Addressing Social Issues in India", endeavors to unravel these complex threads, providing an insightful exploration of the multifaceted challenges and potential solutions that define the nation's social landscape.

The introductory section sets the stage, offering a panoramic view of the varied social issues that India grapples with. From entrenched poverty to gender-based discrimination, from educational disparities to environmental concerns, the subsequent sections delve into the heart of these issues, unraveling their intricacies and examining the myriad ways in which individuals and institutions are striving for positive change.

Government policies wield considerable influence in shaping the social contours of the nation. One section scrutinizes the role of governmental interventions, assessing their impact on communities and examining the areas where policy measures have succeeded or faltered. Yet, the transformative potential of change often emerges from the grassroots. Another section illuminates the invaluable contributions of non-governmental organizations and grassroots movements as catalysts for social change.

Media, as a powerful force shaping public perceptions, is the focus of a dedicated section. This section delves into the role of media in influencing social narratives and explores its potential to be a force for positive change. The subsequent sections spotlight the power of youth activism, the persistence of poverty, and the pursuit of educational equity - each showcasing the struggles, triumphs, and ongoing efforts to address these critical social issues.

As we traverse this comprehensive exploration, we encounter sections dedicated to the intricacies of gender inequality, the historical legacy of the caste system, and the delicate balance between religious harmony and intolerance. Sections on healthcare, environmental stewardship, corruption, child labor, human trafficking, LGBTQ+ rights, and the challenges of urbanization contribute to a holistic understanding of the socio-cultural, economic, and political landscapes that shape the Indian experience.

This book does not merely dwell on the challenges but also looks forward to the future. One section contemplates the prospects of building an inclusive India, examining emerging trends and ongoing initiatives that strive for a more equitable society. The concluding section charts paths to a better tomorrow, reflecting on the collective efforts, challenges, and potential solutions discussed throughout the book, and proposing a vision for a socially just and inclusive India.

In presenting this compendium, our aim is to foster a deeper understanding of the complexities inherent in addressing social issues in India. The narratives within these pages invite readers to contemplate not only the challenges but also the resilience, courage, and innovation exhibited by individuals and communities in the pursuit of a better and more inclusive future for all.

C. P. Kumar
Reiki Healer & Author
Former Scientist 'G', National Institute of Hydrology
Roorkee - 247667, India
Web: https://www.angelfire.com/nh/cpkumar/virgo.html

Chapter 1. Introduction to Social Issues in India

India, a land of rich cultural heritage and diversity, has made significant strides in various fields over the years. However, as the nation progresses, it grapples with an array of social issues that impact millions of lives. This chapter serves as a gateway to understanding the multifaceted challenges that define the social landscape of India. From poverty and inequality to gender discrimination and communal tensions, the nation faces a complex tapestry of issues that require nuanced solutions. This article provides an overview of the diverse social challenges that India confronts, highlighting the need for comprehensive strategies to address them.

Poverty and Economic Disparities

1. Poverty as a Persistent Challenge

One of the most pressing social issues in India is poverty. Despite remarkable economic growth, a substantial portion of the population still lives below the poverty line. Rural areas, in particular, bear the brunt of inadequate access to basic necessities, leading to a cycle of deprivation that spans generations. The challenge lies not only in poverty alleviation but also in ensuring sustainable economic opportunities that uplift communities over the long term.

2. Growing Economic Disparities

While India has witnessed economic growth, the benefits have not been uniformly distributed. Economic disparities between different states, urban and rural areas, and various social groups have widened. This growing gap poses a threat to social cohesion and necessitates policies that promote inclusive growth.

Education and Illiteracy

1. Education as a Tool for Empowerment

Education is a powerful instrument for social transformation. However, India grapples with significant challenges in ensuring universal access to quality education. Disparities in educational opportunities persist, particularly in rural and marginalized communities. Addressing this issue requires not only improving infrastructure but also tackling societal norms that may hinder educational pursuits, especially for girls.

2. The Menace of Illiteracy

Illiteracy remains a formidable obstacle to individual and societal progress. Despite numerous initiatives, a considerable percentage of the population lacks basic literacy skills. Overcoming this challenge demands a holistic approach that includes not just formal education but also adult literacy programs and awareness campaigns.

Gender Discrimination and Women's Empowerment

1. Deep-Seated Gender Inequality

India continues to grapple with deep-seated gender discrimination. From unequal access to education and employment opportunities to pervasive issues like child marriage and dowry, women face multifaceted challenges. Addressing gender inequality is crucial not just for women's rights but also for the overall development of the nation.

2. Empowering Women for Societal Progress

Empowering women is not only a moral imperative but also an economic necessity. Efforts to enhance women's participation in the workforce, eliminate gender-based violence, and challenge societal norms that perpetuate discrimination are essential for building a more equitable society.

Caste Discrimination and Social Stratification

1. The Legacy of Caste System

The caste system, deeply ingrained in Indian society, continues to perpetuate discrimination and social stratification. Despite constitutional safeguards, caste-based discrimination remains a significant challenge, affecting access to education, employment, and even basic human rights.

2. Moving Towards Social Equality

Addressing caste discrimination requires not just legal measures but also a societal shift in attitudes. Affirmative action policies, along with grassroots initiatives, play a crucial role in creating a more egalitarian society. Promoting social harmony and understanding is equally important to break the shackles of centuries-old prejudices.

Healthcare Disparities

1. Challenges in Healthcare Access

Access to healthcare remains a major concern, especially in rural and underserved areas. Limited infrastructure, inadequate healthcare facilities, and a shortage of medical professionals contribute to disparities in health outcomes. The COVID-19 pandemic has further underscored the need for a robust and inclusive healthcare system.

2. Tackling Health Inequities

Improving healthcare in India requires a comprehensive approach that includes infrastructure development, increased healthcare spending, and initiatives to raise awareness about preventive healthcare measures. Addressing social determinants of health, such as poverty and education, is also integral to achieving meaningful progress in this area.

Communal Tensions and Religious Harmony

1. Historical Roots of Communal Tensions

India's history is marked by instances of communal tensions, often fueled by religious and cultural differences. While the constitution guarantees freedom of religion, periodic outbreaks of violence and discord pose challenges to the nation's unity and harmony.

2. Promoting Religious Pluralism

Fostering religious harmony requires a multifaceted approach encompassing education, dialogue, and legal measures. Encouraging interfaith understanding, addressing the root causes of communal tensions, and promoting secular values are crucial for building a society where individuals of all faiths coexist peacefully.

Environmental Sustainability

1. Balancing Development and Environmental Conservation

Rapid industrialization and urbanization have taken a toll on India's environment. From air and water pollution to deforestation, the ecological challenges are manifold. Achieving sustainable development requires a delicate balance between economic growth and environmental conservation.

2. The Role of Community Engagement

Environmental sustainability necessitates active participation from communities. Initiatives promoting sustainable practices, afforestation drives, and awareness campaigns on the impact of climate change are vital components of the solution. Government policies that prioritize environmental conservation and corporate responsibility also play a pivotal role in mitigating these challenges.

Conclusion

India's social fabric is intricately woven with diverse challenges that demand comprehensive and inclusive solutions. This introductory overview scratches the surface of the myriad issues faced by the nation. As we delve deeper into the subsequent chapters of "Addressing Social Issues in India", it is imperative to recognize the interconnected nature of these challenges and work towards holistic solutions that leave no segment of society behind. By understanding, acknowledging, and actively working to resolve these issues, India can pave the way for a more just, equitable, and prosperous future for all its citizens.

Chapter 2. Government Policies and Social Impact

Introduction

In the diverse tapestry of Indian society, social issues have been a persistent challenge, affecting various communities across the nation. The role of government policies in addressing these issues cannot be overstated. This article delves into the nuanced relationship between government policies and their social impact, shedding light on the multifaceted nature of this interaction.

Historical Context of Social Issues in India

To understand the efficacy of government policies, it's essential to explore the historical context of social issues in India. Centuries-old challenges such as caste discrimination, poverty, gender inequality, and inadequate healthcare have deep roots. Government policies have evolved over time in response to these challenges, reflecting the changing dynamics of society.

Caste-Based Reservations and Affirmative Action

One of the most significant interventions by the Indian government has been the implementation of caste-based reservations and affirmative action policies. Initially introduced to address historical injustices and uplift marginalized communities, these policies have played a crucial role in providing educational and employment opportunities. However, the impact has been a subject of debate, with concerns about perpetuating caste divisions and the need for a more nuanced approach.

Economic Policies and Poverty Alleviation

India's economic policies have aimed at reducing poverty and bridging socio-economic disparities. Initiatives such as the Mahatma Gandhi National Rural Employment Guarantee Act (MGNREGA) and targeted subsidy programs have sought to provide economic stability to vulnerable communities. Assessing the efficacy of these policies involves evaluating both short-term relief and long-term empowerment strategies.

Healthcare Policies and Public Health

The impact of government policies on public health is a critical aspect of social well-being. The National Health Mission and Ayushman Bharat initiatives illustrate the government's commitment to improving healthcare accessibility. Analyzing their effectiveness requires examining factors such as infrastructure development, preventive measures, and community awareness.

Education Policies and Empowerment

Education is often regarded as a powerful tool for social change. Government policies in India have focused on increasing literacy rates, promoting inclusive education, and addressing gender disparities. The Right to Education Act is a landmark policy in this regard. Evaluating its impact involves considering enrollment rates, quality of education, and the socio-economic background of students.

Women Empowerment Policies

Gender inequality remains a pervasive social issue in India. Various government initiatives, such as Beti Bachao, Beti

Padhao and the implementation of laws like the Protection of Women from Domestic Violence Act, aim to empower women. Assessing their impact requires a comprehensive examination of changes in societal attitudes, economic opportunities for women, and the effectiveness of legal frameworks.

Environmental Policies and Sustainable Development

Social issues are intricately linked to environmental challenges. Government policies addressing environmental concerns, such as pollution control measures and renewable energy promotion, have social implications. An analysis of these policies involves understanding their impact on community health, livelihoods, and the overall quality of life.

Challenges in Policy Implementation

While policies may be well-intentioned, their impact can be hindered by challenges in implementation. Bureaucratic inefficiencies, corruption, and lack of awareness among the target population are significant hurdles. An examination of these challenges is crucial in understanding why certain policies may fall short of achieving their intended social impact.

Community Participation and Grassroots Initiatives

Effective policy implementation often requires active participation from the communities themselves. Government policies that encourage grassroots initiatives and community involvement tend to have a more sustained impact. Analyzing successful case studies where communities actively engaged in the implementation process provides valuable insights into the dynamics of social change.

Technology and Social Impact Assessment

In the digital age, technology plays a pivotal role in assessing the social impact of government policies. Data analytics, social media, and other technological tools enable real-time monitoring and evaluation. Examining how technology is integrated into the assessment process provides a glimpse into the evolving methods of policy impact analysis.

Conclusion

The intricate relationship between government policies and their social impact in India is a dynamic and evolving field. As the nation grapples with persistent social issues, continuous evaluation and refinement of policies become imperative. This article has aimed to provide a comprehensive overview of the multifaceted aspects involved in understanding the role of government policies in addressing social issues, emphasizing the need for a holistic and inclusive approach for sustainable social development in India.

Introduction

In the diverse landscape of India, social issues have persisted for centuries, ranging from poverty and inequality to lack of access to education and healthcare. Non-Governmental Organizations (NGOs) and grassroots movements have emerged as crucial catalysts for change, playing a pivotal role in addressing and mitigating these challenges. This article delves into the significant contributions of NGOs and grassroots movements in India, examining their impact on various social issues.

The Genesis of NGOs and Grassroots Movements in India

NGOs and grassroots movements in India trace their roots back to the early 20th century. The national struggle for independence provided the fertile ground for the development of these organizations, which initially focused on addressing immediate social issues arising from colonial rule. Post-independence, their scope expanded to encompass a myriad of social challenges affecting the masses.

Education and Empowerment

1. Bridging Educational Gaps

NGOs have been instrumental in bridging the educational divide in India. Initiatives such as Teach For India and

Pratham have been at the forefront of providing quality education to underprivileged children. By working closely with communities, these organizations ensure that education is accessible to all, irrespective of socio-economic backgrounds.

2. Skill Development and Vocational Training

Grassroots movements often focus on skill development and vocational training to empower individuals economically. Organizations like SEWA (Self-Employed Women's Association) have empowered women in rural areas by providing them with training in various crafts and trades, enabling them to become financially independent.

Healthcare Access and Awareness

1. Community Health Programs

Community health programs in India play a crucial role in addressing healthcare challenges at the grassroots level. These initiatives aim to improve the overall well-being of local populations by focusing on preventive measures, maternal and child health, immunization, and sanitation. Through partnerships with government agencies and non-profit organizations, community health programs contribute to building a healthier and more resilient society, particularly in rural and underserved areas where access to healthcare may be limited.

2. Disease Awareness Campaigns

Grassroots movements often engage in raising awareness about prevalent diseases and promoting preventive healthcare practices. The success of campaigns like the Pulse Polio Immunization program and initiatives by organizations like the Indian Cancer Society demonstrates the impact of grassroots efforts in spreading awareness and reducing disease prevalence.

Women's Empowerment and Gender Equality

1. Combating Gender-Based Violence

NGOs in India have been at the forefront of combating gender-based violence. Organizations like Jagori and Vimochana work tirelessly to provide support and legal assistance to victims of domestic violence, sexual harassment, and human trafficking. Through advocacy and awareness programs, these NGOs contribute significantly to the fight for gender equality.

2. Economic Empowerment of Women

Grassroots movements often focus on economic empowerment as a means to address gender disparities. The formation of Self-Help Groups (SHGs) has been a successful model, with organizations like the National Rural Livelihood Mission (NRLM) facilitating the creation of such groups, allowing women to pool resources and engage in income-generating activities.

Environmental Conservation and Sustainable Development

1. Afforestation and Conservation

NGOs play a crucial role in environmental conservation by engaging in afforestation projects and sustainable development initiatives. Organizations like Greenpeace and the Center for Science and Environment work towards raising awareness about climate change, promoting sustainable practices, and holding corporations accountable for their environmental impact.

2. Water Conservation and Sanitation

Grassroots movements often focus on local issues, such as water scarcity and sanitation. The Swachh Bharat Abhiyan, a nationwide cleanliness campaign, saw active participation from grassroots organizations, creating a significant impact on hygiene and sanitation practices in rural and urban areas alike.

Disaster Relief and Rehabilitation

1. Immediate Response and Rehabilitation

NGOs are often the first responders in times of natural disasters. Organizations like Goonj and the Red Cross have been instrumental in providing immediate relief and rehabilitation efforts during earthquakes, floods, and other calamities. Their swift action helps affected communities rebuild their lives and infrastructure.

2. Community Resilience Programs

Grassroots movements contribute to building community resilience through disaster preparedness programs. By educating communities about early warning systems, emergency response, and evacuation plans, these movements empower people to better cope with and mitigate the impact of disasters.

Advocacy and Policy Influence

1. Lobbying for Policy Changes

NGOs play a crucial role in advocating for policy changes that address systemic issues. Through research, lobbying, and collaboration with government bodies, organizations like Amnesty International and Oxfam influence policy decisions that have a direct impact on social issues such as human rights, poverty alleviation, and education.

2. Grassroots Activism and Social Movements

Grassroots movements often fuel larger social movements that shape public opinion and influence policy decisions. Examples include the Chipko Movement for forest conservation and the Narmada Bachao Andolan advocating for the rights of displaced communities. These movements demonstrate the power of collective action in bringing about meaningful change.

Challenges Faced by NGOs and Grassroots Movements

1. Funding Constraints

One of the primary challenges faced by NGOs and grassroots movements is the constant struggle for funding. Reliance on external donors and limited financial resources often hinder the scalability and sustainability of their projects.

2. Bureaucratic Hurdles

NGOs often face bureaucratic hurdles in obtaining permissions and approvals for their projects. Complex regulatory frameworks and red tape can impede the timely implementation of initiatives, affecting their overall effectiveness.

Conclusion

NGOs and grassroots movements stand as indispensable pillars in addressing social issues in India. Their tireless efforts in education, healthcare, women's empowerment, environmental conservation, disaster relief, and advocacy have significantly contributed to positive change. Despite facing challenges, these organizations persist in their mission to create a more equitable and just society, highlighting the profound impact that collective action can have on addressing social challenges in India. As we move forward, recognizing and supporting the work of NGOs and grassroots movements becomes paramount for sustained social development and progress.

Introduction

In the dynamic landscape of India, where diversity and complexity define social structures, the media plays a pivotal role in shaping narratives that influence public perceptions and drive social change. This article explores the multifaceted impact of media in addressing social issues in India. It delves into the power of media to shape public opinions, the responsibility it carries in reflecting societal realities, and its potential in driving positive transformations.

The Power of Narrative Construction

One of the primary functions of media is to construct narratives that provide a lens through which individuals perceive the world around them. Through news articles, television programs, and digital content, the media has the power to highlight specific issues, set agendas, and frame discussions. In India, media narratives often influence public discourse on critical social issues such as poverty, gender inequality, caste discrimination, and communal tensions.

However, it's essential to acknowledge the inherent subjectivity in narrative construction. Media outlets, driven by their own biases, political affiliations, or economic interests, can inadvertently shape narratives that may not accurately represent the complexities of social issues. This raises questions about the objectivity of media and its potential to perpetuate stereotypes, reinforce biases, or even marginalize certain voices.

Reflecting Societal Realities

The media serves as a mirror reflecting the realities of society. It has the power to bring attention to pressing social problems that might otherwise go unnoticed. In India, where socio-economic disparities are widespread, media acts as a bridge between privileged and marginalized communities. Through investigative journalism and human-interest stories, media platforms have the ability to shed light on issues such as rural poverty, healthcare disparities, and educational challenges.

However, the effectiveness of media in reflecting societal realities is contingent upon its commitment to unbiased reporting. Sensationalism, clickbait culture, and the prioritization of entertainment over news with substance can dilute the media's ability to address social issues meaningfully.

Sensationalism is the use of exaggerated or sensational language, images, or content to provoke strong emotional reactions and capture attention, often at the expense of accuracy or objectivity. *Clickbait culture* is a digital media environment where content creators prioritize creating sensational or misleading headlines and thumbnails to attract clicks, views, or engagement, often without delivering substantive or accurate information.

Striking a balance between engaging content and responsible journalism is crucial for ensuring that the media accurately represents the diverse realities of Indian society.

Influencing Public Perceptions

Media holds significant sway over public perceptions, shaping the way individuals view and interpret social issues. The constant bombardment of information through various channels contributes to the formation of opinions, attitudes, and beliefs. For instance, the portrayal of certain communities, events, or policies in a particular light can influence public sentiment and contribute to the formation of stereotypes.

In the Indian context, media has played a pivotal role in shaping perceptions on issues like communal harmony, reservation policies, and cultural diversity. However, the responsibility of the media to provide balanced and nuanced coverage becomes paramount. Biased reporting, sensationalism, and the dissemination of misinformation can have far-reaching consequences, exacerbating social tensions and hindering constructive dialogue.

The Role of Social Media

In the digital age, the rise of social media has revolutionized the dissemination of information and the dynamics of public discourse. Platforms like Facebook, Twitter, and Instagram serve as powerful tools for shaping social narratives, allowing individuals to express their opinions and participate in conversations on a global scale. Social media has proven instrumental in mobilizing movements, amplifying marginalized voices, and holding those in power accountable.

However, the democratization of information on social media comes with its own set of challenges. The spread of fake news, echo chambers that reinforce existing beliefs, and the manipulation of public opinion through targeted campaigns are issues that demand scrutiny. While social media has the potential to be a force for positive social change, it also requires responsible usage and vigilant oversight to mitigate its negative impacts.

Promoting Social Change

Media, as a catalyst for change, has the power to influence public opinion and drive transformative initiatives. Whether through documentaries, investigative journalism, or advocacy campaigns, media can bring about awareness and mobilize communities towards positive action. In India, numerous instances highlight the media's role in catalyzing change, such as campaigns against gender-based violence, environmental degradation, and corruption.

However, the effectiveness of media in promoting social change is contingent upon its ability to go beyond surface-level reporting. In-depth analysis, investigative journalism, and sustained coverage are essential for fostering a deep understanding of the root causes of social issues. Additionally, media organizations need to collaborate with grassroots movements, NGOs, and policymakers to ensure that their efforts translate into tangible societal transformations.

Challenges and Ethical Considerations

While media can be a potent force for social change, it faces several challenges and ethical considerations. Commercial pressures, political influences, and the quest for higher ratings can compromise the integrity of journalistic practices. In India, where media ownership is often concentrated in the hands of a few, the risk of biased reporting and the suppression of dissenting voices is heightened.

Furthermore, the portrayal of vulnerable communities and individuals requires a heightened sense of ethical responsibility. Sensationalism, voyeuristic reporting, and the violation of privacy can perpetuate harm and hinder the very social change that media aims to achieve.

Voyeuristic reporting is a style of journalism characterized by an intrusive focus on sensational and personal details of individuals' lives, often for entertainment value rather than genuine news relevance. This type of reporting tends to prioritize sensationalism and the gratification of curiosity over journalistic integrity and ethical considerations.

Striking a balance between the need for engaging content and ethical considerations is crucial for the media to maintain its credibility and impact.

Conclusion

In addressing social issues in India, the role of media is both influential and complex. Its power to shape narratives, reflect societal realities, influence public perceptions, and drive positive change is unparalleled. However, this power comes with great responsibility. Media organizations must prioritize ethical journalism, unbiased reporting, and a commitment to amplifying diverse voices.

As India continues to grapple with multifaceted social challenges, the media's role in fostering understanding, empathy, and actionable change becomes increasingly significant. By acknowledging its potential pitfalls and actively working towards a more inclusive and responsible media landscape, the industry can contribute meaningfully to the ongoing dialogue on social issues in India.

Introduction

In the diverse tapestry of India, the voices and actions of the youth resonate as powerful catalysts for societal transformation. The emergence of youth activism has ushered in a new era, where young individuals are taking charge, challenging norms, and driving positive change across various social issues. This article delves into the multifaceted role played by young activists in addressing social issues in India.

Understanding Youth Activism

Youth activism is not merely a display of youthful exuberance; it is a conscientious effort by the younger generation to engage with and influence social, political, and environmental spheres. In India, a country grappling with a myriad of social challenges, the youth have stepped forward as change-makers, wielding their passion, energy, and digital prowess to bring about tangible improvements.

The Digital Revolution and Activism

The advent of the digital age has significantly altered the landscape of activism. Social media platforms, in particular, have become powerful tools for young activists to amplify their voices, connect with like-minded individuals, and mobilize support. Through hashtags, viral campaigns, and online petitions, the youth are breaking barriers and reaching a global audience, fostering a sense of unity in addressing social issues.

1. Environmental Activism

One of the pressing concerns that the youth are actively addressing is environmental degradation. Young activists are at the forefront of climate change movements, advocating for sustainable practices, conservation, and policy changes. Through initiatives like tree planting drives, beach clean-ups, and awareness campaigns, these activists are not only fostering a sense of environmental responsibility but also holding policymakers accountable for their actions.

2. Gender Equality

The fight for gender equality has found ardent supporters among the youth. Young activists are challenging patriarchal norms, advocating for equal opportunities, and combating gender-based violence. Through initiatives like workshops on consent, awareness campaigns against dowry, and promoting inclusivity, young activists are striving to create a society where individuals are judged on merit rather than gender.

3. LGBTQ+ Rights

The LGBTQ+ rights movement has gained momentum with the active participation of young activists who are challenging discriminatory laws and societal prejudices. Through pride marches, online campaigns, and support groups, these activists are fostering inclusivity and acceptance. The youth are reshaping narratives around gender and sexuality, promoting a more tolerant and diverse society.

4. Education and Youth Empowerment

Access to quality education remains a significant challenge in many parts of India. Young activists are working towards bridging this gap by initiating projects that provide educational resources, scholarships, and mentorship programs. By empowering underprivileged youth through education, these activists aim to break the cycle of poverty and contribute to the nation's development.

5. Healthcare Advocacy

In the wake of the COVID-19 pandemic, healthcare has become a focal point for youth activism. Young individuals are involved in awareness campaigns, fundraising for medical resources, and volunteering in healthcare facilities. Their resilience and innovation have played a crucial role in addressing health crises and advocating for a more robust healthcare system.

Challenges Faced by Youth Activists

While the impact of youth activism is undeniable, it is essential to acknowledge the challenges faced by young change-makers. Limited resources, societal resistance, and the lack of institutional support can hinder the effectiveness of their initiatives. However, the resilience and determination of these activists often serve as catalysts for change, inspiring others to join the cause.

The Role of Education in Fostering Activism

Education plays a pivotal role in shaping the perspectives and ideologies of the youth. Schools and universities have become breeding grounds for activism, nurturing critical thinking and social consciousness. By integrating social issues into the curriculum and providing platforms for open dialogue, educational institutions contribute to the development of socially responsible citizens.

Conclusion

In the tapestry of addressing social issues in India, the role of youth activists stands out as a vibrant thread, weaving stories of resilience, innovation, and change. The passion and dedication of these young individuals are reshaping the narrative, challenging age-old norms, and inspiring others to join the movement. As India navigates the complexities of the 21st century, the torchbearers of youth activism illuminate the path towards a more inclusive, equitable, and compassionate society.

Introduction

Poverty is a persistent and pervasive issue that has haunted societies across the globe for centuries. In the context of India, a country with a rich cultural heritage and economic potential, the battle against poverty remains a challenging endeavor. This article delves into the causes and consequences of poverty in India while exploring potential solutions to address this deeply rooted social issue.

Understanding Poverty in India

1. Historical Perspective

Poverty in India has historical roots, dating back to the colonial era when exploitation and resource depletion left a lasting impact on the socio-economic structure. Post-independence, efforts were made to eradicate poverty, but progress has been slow and uneven.

2. Economic Disparities

One of the primary contributors to poverty in India is the glaring economic disparity. The divide between the rich and poor has widened, with a significant portion of the population struggling to access basic necessities. Lack of equitable distribution of resources perpetuates poverty.

3. Rural-Urban Divide

The rural-urban disparity is another dimension of poverty. Rural areas often lack access to education, healthcare, and employment opportunities, forcing many to migrate to urban centers in search of a better life. However, urban areas present their own set of challenges, such as high living costs and intense competition for jobs.

Causes of Poverty in India

1. Unemployment and Underemployment

High levels of unemployment and underemployment contribute significantly to poverty. A large portion of the population is engaged in low-paying, informal jobs, leading to insufficient income to meet basic needs. Lack of skill development and inadequate job creation exacerbate the problem.

2. Lack of Education

Education is a powerful tool for breaking the cycle of poverty, yet a significant portion of the Indian population faces barriers to accessing quality education. This perpetuates a cycle where individuals are unable to acquire the skills necessary for higher-paying jobs, trapping them in a cycle of poverty.

3. Healthcare Challenges

Poor health exacerbates the challenges faced by those in poverty. Limited access to healthcare facilities, lack of awareness, and inadequate nutrition contribute to a cycle of illness and economic hardship. High medical expenses can push families further into poverty.

4. Social Discrimination

Discrimination based on caste, gender, and religion remains a significant obstacle to social progress. Marginalized communities face limited opportunities and unequal access to resources, creating a vicious cycle of poverty that is difficult to break.

Consequences of Poverty

1. Impact on Health

Poverty has a direct correlation with poor health outcomes. Limited access to nutritious food, clean water, and healthcare services lead to higher rates of malnutrition, diseases, and infant mortality. This not only affects individuals but has broader implications for the overall health of the nation.

2. Educational Challenges

The lack of financial resources often prevents children from impoverished families from attending school. This perpetuates the cycle of poverty as limited education opportunities hinder the development of skills necessary for economic empowerment.

3. Economic Stagnation

Poverty hampers economic growth by limiting the potential of a significant portion of the population. When large segments of society are unable to contribute effectively to the workforce, it constrains the overall productivity and progress of the nation.

4. Social Unrest

Persistent poverty can lead to social unrest and instability. Frustration and despair among the impoverished population can manifest in protests, crime, and a general breakdown of social cohesion. Addressing poverty is, therefore, crucial for maintaining social harmony.

Solutions to Alleviate Poverty

1. Education Reforms

Implementing comprehensive education reforms is essential for breaking the cycle of poverty. This includes ensuring access to quality education in rural areas, vocational training programs, and initiatives to eliminate barriers based on gender and socio-economic status.

2. Employment Generation

Addressing unemployment requires a multi-pronged approach. Encouraging entrepreneurship, promoting small and medium-sized enterprises, and investing in skill development programs can create avenues for sustainable employment and income generation.

3. Healthcare Access

Improving healthcare infrastructure and ensuring universal access to medical services are critical steps in alleviating poverty. Prevention-focused initiatives, such as vaccination programs and awareness campaigns, can contribute to better overall health outcomes.

4. Social Equality

Tackling social discrimination is fundamental to addressing poverty. Implementing policies that promote equality, inclusivity, and affirmative action can help uplift marginalized communities, providing them with equal opportunities to thrive.

5. Agricultural Reforms

Given the significant portion of the population dependent on agriculture, reforms in the agricultural sector are crucial. This includes implementing sustainable farming practices, providing farmers with access to modern technology, and ensuring fair pricing for agricultural produce.

Conclusion

In addressing the persistent struggle against poverty in India, a comprehensive and multi-faceted approach is imperative. Economic reforms, social initiatives, and targeted interventions are all integral components of a strategy aimed at breaking the cycle of poverty. By understanding the causes, acknowledging the consequences, and actively working towards sustainable solutions, India can pave the way for a more equitable and prosperous future. The battle against poverty is a collective responsibility that requires the concerted efforts of government, civil society, and the private sector to ensure lasting change.

Introduction

Education is often hailed as the cornerstone of a nation's progress, empowering individuals and fostering societal development. However, the stark reality in India reveals a landscape marked by educational inequities, where access to quality education remains a distant dream for many. This article delves into the multifaceted aspects of educational disparities in India and explores the ongoing efforts to bridge the learning gap, striving for a more inclusive and equitable educational system.

Understanding Educational Disparities

1. Regional Disparities

One of the prominent challenges contributing to educational inequities in India is the stark regional divide. Urban areas often boast well-equipped schools with qualified teachers, while rural counterparts grapple with inadequate infrastructure and a shortage of skilled educators. This geographical imbalance widens the education gap, limiting opportunities for students in less privileged regions.

2. Economic Disparities

Economic inequalities perpetuate educational disparities, with families in lower income brackets struggling to afford even basic educational necessities. The cost of textbooks, uniforms, and transportation often becomes a formidable barrier, hindering the educational journey of countless children. This economic divide manifests in unequal access to quality schools, extracurricular activities, and educational resources.

3. Gender Disparities

Despite significant strides, gender-based educational disparities persist in India. Deep-rooted societal norms and biases often limit educational opportunities for girls, particularly in certain regions. Early marriage, social expectations, and safety concerns contribute to the lower enrollment and higher dropout rates among female students, perpetuating gender-based educational inequities.

Efforts to Promote Accessibility and Quality

1. Government Initiatives

The government has implemented various initiatives to address educational inequities. Schemes like Sarva Shiksha Abhiyan and Right to Education aim to provide free and compulsory education to all children. These programs focus on improving infrastructure, ensuring teacher availability, and promoting inclusivity, especially in marginalized communities.

2. Digital Education Revolution

In the wake of the digital age, there is a growing emphasis on leveraging technology to bridge educational gaps. The Digital India initiative seeks to make technology an integral part of the education system. Online learning platforms, digital textbooks, and e-learning resources aim to provide equitable access to educational content, transcending geographical barriers.

3. Community-Based Interventions

Several non-governmental organizations and community-driven initiatives play a pivotal role in addressing educational inequities. These organizations often work closely with local communities to identify specific needs, provide educational support, and create awareness about the importance of education. Grassroots efforts contribute significantly to fostering a sense of ownership and participation in education.

4. Scholarship Programs

To alleviate economic barriers, scholarship programs have been instrumental in providing financial assistance to deserving students. These programs, whether sponsored by the government or private institutions, aim to make education more accessible by covering tuition fees, purchasing study materials, and supporting students from economically disadvantaged backgrounds.

Challenges and Roadblocks

1. Infrastructure Challenges

Despite commendable efforts, infrastructure challenges persist in many parts of the country. Schools in remote areas often lack proper buildings, sanitation facilities, and basic resources, impeding the learning experience for students. Addressing these infrastructure gaps is crucial for ensuring a conducive learning environment.

2. Teacher Shortages

A shortage of qualified and motivated teachers remains a significant impediment to quality education. In remote areas, attracting and retaining skilled educators is challenging, resulting in a compromised learning experience for students. Addressing teacher shortages involves not only recruitment but also ongoing professional development and support.

3. Socio-Cultural Barriers

Socio-cultural factors, deeply ingrained in certain communities, pose challenges to educational equity. Prevailing attitudes towards caste, gender, and occupation can influence educational choices and opportunities. Overcoming these barriers requires a comprehensive approach, involving community engagement, awareness campaigns, and policy interventions.

4. Digital Divide

While digital education initiatives show promise, the digital divide remains a substantial challenge. Many students, especially in rural and economically disadvantaged areas, lack access to the necessary devices and reliable internet connectivity. Bridging this divide is crucial for ensuring that the benefits of technology in education reach all corners of the country.

Future Perspectives

1. Holistic Reforms

A comprehensive overhaul of the education system is imperative to address deeply rooted inequities. Reforms should encompass curriculum changes, teacher training programs, and infrastructural improvements, fostering an inclusive learning environment that caters to the diverse needs of students across regions and backgrounds.

2. Community Engagement

Empowering local communities to actively participate in the educational process is key to sustainable change. Community-driven initiatives should be encouraged, and partnerships between schools, NGOs, and local authorities can contribute to creating a supportive ecosystem for education.

3. Technology Integration

Continued efforts to bridge the digital divide are essential for harnessing the potential of technology in education. Initiatives like providing affordable devices, expanding internet connectivity, and creating digital literacy programs can help ensure that no student is left behind in the digital era.

4. Policy Advocacy

Advocacy for policy changes that address the root causes of educational inequities is crucial. This includes addressing economic disparities, challenging societal norms, and ensuring that educational policies are designed with inclusivity in mind. A collective effort from policymakers, educators, and civil society is necessary to drive systemic change.

Conclusion

Educational inequities in India are complex and deeply rooted, requiring concerted efforts from various stakeholders to bring about meaningful change. While progress has been made through government initiatives, community-driven interventions, and technological advancements, challenges persist. Bridging the learning gap necessitates a holistic and sustained approach, encompassing policy reforms, community engagement, and the judicious use of technology. As India continues its journey towards social progress, addressing educational disparities remains a crucial step in building a more equitable and inclusive society.

Introduction

Gender inequality remains a pervasive and deeply rooted social issue in India, impacting millions of lives across the country. Despite strides towards modernization and economic growth, the shackles of gender-based discrimination persist in various forms. This article delves into the roots of gender inequality in India and examines the initiatives that are challenging these ingrained norms, aiming to pave the way for a more equitable society.

Understanding the Roots

1. Cultural Norms and Stereotypes

India's rich cultural tapestry is often marred by traditional norms and stereotypes that reinforce gender roles. Deeply ingrained societal expectations dictate the behavior and opportunities available to individuals based on their gender. The perception of women as homemakers and caregivers, while men are seen as breadwinners, contributes to a hierarchical structure that limits women's participation in various spheres of life.

2. Educational Disparities

Access to education is a critical factor in shaping perceptions and dismantling gender-based discrimination. However, in many parts of India, particularly in rural areas, girls still face challenges in accessing quality education. The prevalence of early marriages and societal biases against educating girls perpetuates a cycle of ignorance, limiting their future prospects.

3. Economic Disparities

Economic opportunities for women remain limited, further exacerbating gender inequality. Wage gaps persist, and women are often concentrated in lower-paying and less prestigious occupations. The lack of financial independence can make women vulnerable to various forms of exploitation and reinforces the power dynamics that perpetuate gender discrimination.

Initiatives for Gender Equality

1. Educational Reforms

Recognizing the pivotal role education plays in challenging gender norms, various initiatives have been launched to improve access to education for girls. Scholarships, infrastructure development, and awareness campaigns aim to break down barriers and create an environment where girls can pursue education without fear or societal constraints.

2. Legal Reforms and Women's Empowerment

Legislative measures have been implemented to address gender-based discrimination, such as laws against dowry, domestic violence, and workplace harassment. Additionally, initiatives promoting women's empowerment, such as financial literacy programs and skill development initiatives, are instrumental in fostering economic independence.

3. Corporate Initiatives for Gender Diversity

The corporate sector plays a crucial role in shaping societal norms. Many companies in India are actively working towards fostering gender diversity in the workplace. Policies promoting equal pay, maternity leave, and flexible work hours contribute to creating a more inclusive work environment. Corporate social responsibility initiatives are also directed towards uplifting women in communities through skill-building programs and entrepreneurship support.

4. Media Influence and Awareness Campaigns

Recognizing the power of media in shaping perceptions, awareness campaigns have been launched to challenge gender stereotypes. Advertisements, movies, and television shows that promote gender equality and showcase women in diverse roles contribute to changing societal attitudes.

5. NGO Interventions and Grassroots Movements

Non-governmental organizations (NGOs) play a vital role in addressing gender inequality at the grassroots level. These organizations often work directly with communities, providing support, education, and resources to empower women. Grassroots movements advocating for women's rights and challenging discriminatory practices contribute to a bottom-up approach in dismantling gender-based discrimination.

Challenges and the Way Forward

1. Resistance to Change

Despite the progress made, there is resistance to change, particularly in conservative pockets of society. Deep-rooted beliefs and patriarchal structures pose significant challenges to initiatives aimed at dismantling gender inequality. Addressing these cultural barriers requires sustained efforts in education and awareness.

2. Implementation of Laws

While there are laws in place to protect women's rights, their effective implementation remains a challenge. Strengthening the judicial system and ensuring that laws are enforced consistently can contribute to creating a safer environment for women and holding perpetrators accountable.

3. Intersectionality

Gender inequality intersects with other forms of discrimination, such as caste, class, and religion. Initiatives addressing gender-based discrimination need to adopt an intersectional approach, recognizing the unique challenges faced by women from marginalized communities.

4. Policy Coherence

Achieving gender equality requires a coherent approach across various policy domains, including education, healthcare, employment, and legal frameworks. Coordinated efforts at the policy level are essential to creating a holistic and sustainable impact.

Conclusion

Gender inequality in India is a multifaceted issue deeply intertwined with cultural norms, educational disparities, and economic imbalances. While numerous initiatives are underway to challenge these inequalities, there is still much work to be done. Breaking the chains of gender-based discrimination requires a comprehensive and collaborative effort involving government bodies, civil society, corporate entities, and individuals. By addressing the roots of gender inequality and fostering initiatives that promote education, empowerment, and awareness, India can aspire to create a society where gender is no longer a determinant of one's opportunities and potential.

Chapter 9. Caste System
Legacy and Struggle

Introduction

The caste system, deeply ingrained in the fabric of Indian society, has left an indelible mark on the country's history and social structure. Its roots can be traced back to ancient scriptures, where social stratification was initially based on one's occupation. Over time, this system evolved into a rigid hierarchy, shaping the lives and opportunities of individuals based on their birth. This article explores the historical context of the caste system, its enduring legacy, and the ongoing struggles to address caste-based discrimination in contemporary India.

Historical Origins of the Caste System

1. Vedic Period

The caste system finds its earliest mention in ancient Indian scriptures, particularly in the Rig Veda, where society was divided into four varnas – Brahmins, Kshatriyas, Vaishyas, and Shudras. Initially, these varnas were associated with distinct duties and responsibilities, emphasizing a division of labor rather than birth-based discrimination.

2. Evolution during the Later Vedic Period

As society progressed, the varna system became more rigid, with birth determining one's place in the hierarchy. The Manusmriti, a key legal text from this period, codified these social divisions, reinforcing the idea that each varna had a specific role to play in maintaining societal order.

3. Emergence of Jatis

The varna system further fragmented into numerous subgroups, known as jatis, based on profession, region, or even social interactions. This sub-division intensified social stratification, creating a complex web of hierarchies that extended beyond the four varnas.

The Caste System in Practice

1. Social and Economic Disparities

The caste system perpetuated social and economic disparities, with the Brahmins enjoying the highest status as priests and scholars, while the Shudras were relegated to menial tasks. This hierarchy restricted mobility and opportunities, leading to the entrenchment of social inequality over centuries.

2. Untouchability and Outcastes

The lowest stratum of the caste system was occupied by those considered "untouchables" or Dalits. They faced severe discrimination, often barred from entering temples, drawing water from common wells, and participating in social events. This dehumanizing practice continued for generations, creating a marginalized community that struggled for basic human rights.

Caste System and Religion

1. Justification through Religion

The caste system found justification in religious texts, leading to the entwining of social hierarchy with spiritual beliefs. Many argued that the varna one was born into was a result of karma from past lives, creating a fatalistic acceptance of one's social position.

2. Reform Movements

Amidst the perpetuation of caste-based discrimination, various reform movements emerged over the centuries, challenging the rigid social order. Visionaries like Raja Ram Mohan Roy, Jyotirao Phule, and B.R. Ambedkar played pivotal roles in advocating for social justice and equality, pushing for reforms within religious and societal structures.

Contemporary Efforts to Address Caste Discrimination

1. Constitutional Safeguards

Post-independence, the framers of the Indian Constitution recognized the need to address historical injustices and laid the foundation for an egalitarian society. Affirmative action measures, such as reservations in education and employment, were instituted to uplift marginalized communities, particularly Scheduled Castes (SCs) and Scheduled Tribes (STs).

2. Legal Measures

Several legislative acts, such as the Protection of Civil Rights Act (1955) and the Scheduled Castes and Scheduled Tribes (Prevention of Atrocities) Act (1989), were enacted to curb caste-based discrimination and violence. These laws provide a legal framework for prosecuting offenses committed against marginalized communities.

3. Social Movements

Contemporary India has witnessed a surge in social movements advocating for the rights of Dalits and other marginalized groups. Movements like the Dalit Panthers and the Bhim Army have actively worked to raise awareness, challenge discriminatory practices, and empower the oppressed.

Challenges and Persistent Discrimination

1. Deep-Rooted Social Attitudes

Despite legislative measures and social movements, deep-rooted social attitudes and prejudices continue to perpetuate caste discrimination. Inter-caste marriages, for example, are often met with resistance, reflecting the enduring grip of the caste system on the psyche of Indian society.

2. Economic Disparities

While affirmative action has made strides in addressing educational and employment disparities, economic inequalities persist. Many Dalits still face economic marginalization, limiting their access to resources and opportunities for upward mobility.

3. Political Dynamics

Caste plays a significant role in Indian politics, influencing voting patterns, candidate selection, and policy decisions. While political representation for marginalized groups has increased, there is a need for sustained efforts to ensure that their voices are not only heard but also translated into meaningful policy changes.

Future Prospects and Conclusion

1. Education and Awareness

Education and awareness are crucial in challenging ingrained prejudices. Initiatives promoting inclusivity in educational curricula and fostering dialogue on caste-related issues can contribute to breaking down societal barriers.

2. Economic Empowerment

Efforts to address economic disparities must go beyond reservations and focus on creating opportunities for skill development and entrepreneurship within marginalized communities. Economic empowerment can pave the way for sustainable social transformation.

3. Social Harmony

Building social harmony requires collective efforts from all sections of society. Dialogues that promote understanding, empathy, and mutual respect are essential for dismantling the divisive mindset perpetuated by the caste system.

Conclusion

The caste system, with its historical origins deeply rooted in Indian society, has left a lasting impact on the country's social fabric. While significant strides have been made in addressing caste discrimination through constitutional safeguards, legal measures, and social movements, challenges persist. The journey toward a caste-free and egalitarian society requires continuous efforts, encompassing education, economic empowerment, and social harmony. Only through a collective and sustained commitment can India hope to overcome the legacy of the caste system and pave the way for a more inclusive and just future.

Chapter 10. Religious Harmony vs. Intolerance

Introduction

India, with its rich tapestry of cultures, languages, and religions, has long been celebrated for its diversity. However, the nation also grapples with the challenge of religious intolerance, which has led to discrimination and tension among various communities. This article delves into the complex issue of religious harmony versus intolerance in India, examining instances of discrimination and exploring potential avenues for fostering a more inclusive and tolerant society.

Historical Context

Understanding the dynamics of religious harmony and intolerance in India requires a glance at its historical context. The country has a history of diverse religious practices, with Hinduism, Islam, Sikhism, Christianity, Buddhism, and Jainism coexisting for centuries. While India has been a land of religious tolerance for much of its history, certain periods have witnessed discord, often fueled by political motivations.

Instances of Religious Discrimination

1. Communal Riots and Violence

One of the most visible manifestations of religious intolerance in India has been communal riots and violence. Throughout the years, instances of clashes between different religious communities have left scars on the social fabric. The Babri Masjid demolition in 1992 and the Gujarat riots in 2002 are stark examples of religious tensions escalating into large-scale violence.

2. Discrimination in Education and Employment

Religious discrimination often extends into educational and employment spheres. Minority communities may face barriers in accessing quality education or securing employment opportunities due to prejudice and bias. This not only hampers the development of individuals but also perpetuates social disparities.

3. Legal Challenges

Despite constitutional guarantees of religious freedom and equality, legal challenges persist. The misuse of anti-conversion laws in some states has been a cause for concern, leading to allegations of targeting religious minorities. Additionally, instances of discriminatory practices, such as denying religious minorities access to public services, highlight systemic challenges that need addressing.

Fostering Religious Harmony

1. Educational Reforms

Promoting religious harmony begins with education. Reforms in the educational system can play a pivotal role in fostering understanding and tolerance among different religious communities. Introducing diverse perspectives in school curricula and encouraging interfaith dialogue can help break down stereotypes and build bridges of understanding.

2. Interfaith Initiatives

Interfaith initiatives are crucial for building relationships among diverse religious communities. Regular dialogues, seminars, and community events that bring people of different faiths together can dispel misconceptions and promote a sense of unity. Interfaith organizations and forums can serve as platforms for open discussions and collaborative efforts.

3. Media Responsibility

The media has a significant influence on shaping public perceptions. Responsible journalism can contribute to religious harmony by avoiding sensationalism and biased reporting. Media outlets should strive to represent diverse religious communities accurately and promote stories that highlight shared values and cooperation.

4. Legal Reforms

Addressing legal challenges is imperative for ensuring religious harmony. Reforms in anti-conversion laws to prevent misuse and stricter enforcement of laws against hate speech and discrimination can contribute to creating a more just and inclusive society. Legal mechanisms should be strengthened to protect the rights of religious minorities and ensure equal opportunities for all.

5. Grassroots Initiatives

Change often begins at the grassroots level. Local community leaders, religious figures, and non-governmental organizations (NGOs) can play a crucial role in promoting religious harmony. Grassroots initiatives that focus on community building, cultural exchange, and collaborative projects can foster a sense of shared humanity and bridge gaps between different religious groups.

Challenges and Opportunities

While the path to religious harmony is riddled with challenges, it also presents opportunities for positive transformation. Recognizing and addressing the root causes of intolerance, whether they be economic disparities, political manipulation, or historical grievances, is essential for building a more harmonious society.

Conclusion

Religious harmony in India is not merely a philosophical ideal but a practical necessity for the nation's social cohesion and progress. By addressing instances of religious discrimination through educational reforms, interfaith initiatives, responsible media practices, legal reforms, and grassroots efforts, India can strive towards fostering an environment where diversity is celebrated, and intolerance becomes a relic of the past. It is through collective efforts, understanding, and empathy that the country can pave the way for a more inclusive and tolerant future, setting an example for the rest of the world to follow.

Chapter 11. Healthcare Access
A Prescription for Change

Introduction

Access to healthcare is a fundamental right that every
individual deserves, yet in a country as diverse as India,
healthcare challenges persistently undermine the well-being
of its population. This article delves into the intricate web
of healthcare issues in India, examining the barriers that
hinder accessibility and proposing comprehensive
strategies for positive change.

The Current Landscape of Healthcare in India

1. Disparities in Healthcare Delivery

One of the primary challenges is the stark contrast between
urban and rural healthcare infrastructure. Urban areas often
enjoy better-equipped hospitals, skilled medical
professionals, and superior medical technologies. On the
contrary, rural regions grapple with inadequate facilities, a
shortage of doctors, and limited access to essential
medicines.

2. Overburdened Public Healthcare System

India's public healthcare system, while aiming to provide
affordable healthcare to all, struggles with overwhelming
patient loads, resulting in long waiting times and
compromised quality of care. This overburdening often
forces citizens to seek private healthcare, creating a divide
between those who can afford it and those who cannot.

Barriers to Healthcare Access

1. Financial Barriers

High out-of-pocket expenses and a lack of comprehensive health insurance coverage leave a significant portion of the population vulnerable to financial hardships. For many, seeking medical treatment means draining savings or taking loans, deterring them from accessing timely healthcare.

2. Geographical Barriers

In a vast country like India, geographical barriers play a pivotal role in limiting healthcare access. Remote areas face challenges related to transportation infrastructure, making it difficult for residents to reach healthcare facilities promptly.

3. Limited Awareness and Education

Healthcare literacy is a critical factor in ensuring timely and appropriate medical interventions. A lack of awareness about preventive healthcare measures, the importance of vaccinations, and the management of chronic diseases contributes to the overall burden on the healthcare system.

Strategies for Healthcare Improvement

1. Strengthening Primary Healthcare Infrastructure

Primary healthcare facilities are first-contact, community-based centers providing essential and basic health services and preventive care. Secondary healthcare facilities are specialized medical centers, including hospitals and clinics, offering more complex diagnostic and treatment services beyond primary care. Tertiary healthcare facilities are high-level medical institutions, such as teaching hospitals, providing specialized and advanced medical services for complex and rare health conditions.

Investing in robust primary healthcare infrastructure can alleviate the burden on secondary and tertiary healthcare facilities. Strengthening community health centers and providing training for local healthcare workers can enhance the delivery of basic healthcare services in rural areas.

2. Leveraging Technology for Telemedicine

Embracing technology, especially in remote areas, can bridge the geographical gap. Telemedicine services can connect patients with healthcare professionals, allowing consultations, diagnostics, and follow-ups without the need for physical presence.

3. Public-Private Partnerships

Collaboration between the public and private sectors can lead to a more comprehensive and accessible healthcare system. Public-private partnerships can address the resource gaps in public healthcare while making private healthcare more affordable through subsidies and regulated pricing.

4. Universal Health Coverage

Implementing a robust universal health coverage system can significantly reduce the financial burden on individuals. By expanding health insurance schemes and ensuring coverage for a broad range of medical treatments, the government can pave the way for equitable healthcare access for all.

5. Empowering Healthcare Workers

Investing in the training and education of healthcare professionals, especially in rural areas, is crucial for enhancing the quality of healthcare services. Initiatives to attract and retain medical professionals in underserved regions can address the urban-rural healthcare divide.

The Role of Education and Awareness

1. Promoting Health Literacy

Educational programs at schools and community levels can empower individuals with the knowledge needed for preventive healthcare. Focusing on hygiene, nutrition, and early disease detection can contribute to a healthier population and reduce the burden on the healthcare system.

2. Community Engagement

Involving communities in healthcare decision-making processes can lead to more effective health policies. Community-based programs for health promotion and disease prevention, along with the active participation of local leaders, can create a sense of ownership and responsibility for community health.

Government Initiatives and Policy Reforms

1. Increased Healthcare Budget Allocation

A significant step towards addressing healthcare challenges involves increasing the government's budget allocation for the health sector. Adequate funding can support the implementation of various initiatives, infrastructure development, and the overall improvement of healthcare services.

2. Regulatory Reforms

Introducing and enforcing policies that regulate the private healthcare sector can ensure fair pricing and quality standards. Stricter regulations can prevent overcharging and unethical practices, making healthcare more affordable and transparent for the public.

3. Monitoring and Evaluation

Implementing robust monitoring and evaluation mechanisms for healthcare programs is essential for assessing their effectiveness. Regular audits and feedback loops can help identify shortcomings, allowing for timely corrections and improvements.

Conclusion

Addressing healthcare challenges in India requires a multi-faceted approach that encompasses infrastructure development, technology integration, community involvement, and policy reforms. By tackling the root causes of disparities in healthcare access, the nation can move towards a more equitable and inclusive healthcare system. As India strives for social progress, ensuring the health and well-being of its citizens should remain a top priority, fostering a society where quality healthcare is a universal right rather than a privilege.

Chapter 12. Environmental Stewardship
Balancing Growth and Conservation

Introduction

India, a land of diverse landscapes and cultures, is at a crossroads where rapid development and environmental conservation intersect. As the nation strives for economic growth, it is imperative to address the pressing environmental issues that accompany this development. This article explores the delicate balance between growth and conservation, emphasizing the need for environmental stewardship in the context of India's social landscape.

The Paradox of Progress

India has made significant strides in economic development, but this progress has come at a cost. The unchecked exploitation of natural resources, deforestation, and pollution have given rise to a myriad of environmental challenges. Air and water quality degradation, loss of biodiversity, and climate change impacts have become stark realities, affecting both urban and rural communities.

Urbanization and Its Toll on the Environment

The rapid urbanization witnessed in India has been a double-edged sword. While cities have become hubs of economic activity, they also generate immense environmental pressure. Unplanned urban growth leads to increased demand for energy, water, and infrastructure, often at the expense of green spaces and ecological balance. The result is a rise in pollution levels, compromised public health, and a strain on natural resources.

Industrialization

The industrial sector, a cornerstone of India's economic progress, contributes significantly to environmental degradation. Untreated industrial effluents, improper waste disposal, and excessive resource consumption pose serious threats. Striking a balance between industrial growth and environmental protection is crucial for sustainable development.

Agriculture

Agriculture, the backbone of the Indian economy, is another sector facing a conundrum. Intensive farming practices, excessive use of chemical fertilizers, and inefficient water management have led to soil degradation and water scarcity. Sustainable agricultural practices are essential to ensure food security without compromising the environment.

Climate Change

India is not immune to the global challenge of climate change. Extreme weather events, rising temperatures, and unpredictable monsoons impact agriculture, biodiversity, and livelihoods. Mitigating climate change requires a comprehensive approach that includes renewable energy adoption, afforestation, and sustainable land-use practices.

Conservation vs. Development

The perceived conflict between conservation and development often pits environmentalists against policymakers and businesses. However, finding common ground is imperative for long-term sustainability. Integrating environmental considerations into development plans, enforcing stringent regulations, and promoting green technologies can bridge the gap between growth and conservation.

Community Involvement

Empowering local communities is integral to achieving environmental stewardship. Engaging communities in conservation efforts not only ensures the protection of natural resources but also fosters a sense of ownership. Traditional ecological knowledge, coupled with modern sustainable practices, can create a harmonious coexistence between communities and their environment.

Policy Reforms

Effective environmental stewardship requires robust policies that prioritize sustainability over short-term gains. Stringent regulations, incentives for eco-friendly practices, and penalties for environmental violations are essential components of a comprehensive policy framework. Policymakers must collaborate with experts, communities, and businesses to formulate and implement measures that balance growth and conservation.

Technological Innovations

Harnessing technology can be a game-changer in environmental stewardship. From renewable energy solutions to waste management technologies, innovation can drive sustainable development. Government and private sectors should invest in research and development to create and adopt technologies that minimize environmental impact without compromising economic growth.

Education and Awareness

Environmental stewardship begins with education and awareness. Ingraining environmental consciousness in educational curricula, raising public awareness campaigns, and promoting eco-friendly practices can foster a culture of sustainability. Informed citizens are more likely to participate actively in conservation efforts and hold authorities accountable for environmental policies.

Conclusion

Balancing growth and conservation in India requires a paradigm shift in the way development is approached. Environmental stewardship is not a choice but a necessity for the nation's long-term well-being. By embracing sustainable practices, involving communities, implementing effective policies, and leveraging technology, India can navigate the path to development without compromising the health of its environment. The choices made today will shape the future, and it is incumbent upon all stakeholders to ensure that progress and conservation go hand in hand for a sustainable and prosperous India.

Introduction

Corruption, a pervasive social issue, has long cast its ominous shadow over India's progress and development. The *Corruption Chronicles* (narrative or series of stories chronicling instances of corruption within India) unfold a labyrinthine narrative that intertwines with the fabric of society, influencing every facet of life. In this article, we delve into the multifaceted impact of corruption on Indian society and explore the various anti-corruption measures in place to navigate the intricate web of dishonest practices.

The Socio-Economic Ramifications

Corruption in India isn't merely a bureaucratic nuisance; its tendrils reach deep into the socio-economic structure, leaving lasting scars. From impeding economic growth to exacerbating income inequality, corruption fosters an environment that hampers the nation's potential. The misallocation of resources, fueled by bribery and nepotism, hinders equitable development, leaving marginalized communities at a perpetual disadvantage.

1. Economic Stagnation

Corruption corrodes the foundation of economic progress. Funds earmarked for developmental projects are siphoned off, and public resources are misused for personal gains. This diverts essential capital away from infrastructure development, healthcare, and education, stalling the country's economic growth.

2. Widening Income Inequality

The impact of corruption is disproportionately felt by the vulnerable sections of society. As illicit deals and bribery become the norm, opportunities for the underprivileged diminish. This exacerbates income inequality, creating a social chasm that separates the haves from the have-nots.

The Erosion of Trust in Institutions

One of the most insidious consequences of corruption is the erosion of trust in public institutions. When citizens perceive the very institutions meant to protect their interests as corrupt, it leads to a crisis of confidence. The judiciary, law enforcement agencies, and government bodies all suffer from this erosion, undermining the democratic foundations of the nation.

1. Judicial Implications

Corruption within the judiciary weakens the core of the legal system. From delayed justice to compromised verdicts, the integrity of the judiciary is compromised, eroding citizens' faith in the rule of law. This has far-reaching consequences for a society striving for justice and equality.

2. Law Enforcement Challenges

Corruption within law enforcement agencies distorts the pursuit of justice. Police officers susceptible to bribes compromise investigations, allowing criminals to escape accountability. This compromises public safety and breeds a culture of impunity.

Grassroots Impact

While corruption is often associated with high-profile cases and political maneuvering, its impact is most acutely felt at the grassroots level. From obtaining basic services to navigating bureaucratic procedures, the common citizen is entangled in a web of corruption that impedes progress and amplifies frustration.

1. Bureaucratic Obstacles

Every interaction with government offices, from obtaining permits to accessing social welfare schemes, is marred by corrupt practices. The bureaucratic machinery becomes a labyrinth of red tape, where citizens are forced to pay bribes for services that should be accessible without such impediments.

2. Educational Challenges

Corruption infiltrates the education system, compromising the quality of education available to the masses. From fraudulent appointments to the manipulation of examination results, the repercussions of corruption in education are profound, perpetuating a cycle of ignorance and hindering social mobility.

Anti-Corruption Measures

Addressing the labyrinth of corruption requires a multifaceted approach. Various anti-corruption measures have been introduced, aiming to curb dishonest practices, rebuild trust in institutions, and foster a culture of transparency.

1. Legislative Reforms

Stringent legislative reforms form the backbone of anti-corruption measures. Acts such as the Prevention of Corruption Act and the Right to Information Act empower citizens to hold public officials accountable. However, the effectiveness of these measures relies heavily on their enforcement and the robustness of the legal system.

2. Whistleblower Protection

Protecting those who expose corruption is vital for creating a culture of accountability. Whistleblower protection laws encourage individuals to come forward with information about corrupt practices without fear of reprisal. Strengthening these protections is crucial to dismantling the culture of silence surrounding corruption.

3. Technology and Transparency

Harnessing technology to enhance transparency is a key strategy in the fight against corruption. E-governance initiatives, online platforms for public services, and digital payment systems reduce the scope for corrupt practices by minimizing human intervention and creating a transparent trail of transactions.

4. Civil Society Participation

Engaging civil society in the fight against corruption is imperative. Non-governmental organizations, advocacy groups, and community-based initiatives play a vital role in raising awareness, holding public officials accountable, and fostering a collective commitment to eradicating corruption.

Conclusion

The Corruption Chronicles in India present a complex narrative of intertwining challenges and potential solutions. The socio-economic ramifications of corruption are profound, affecting the most vulnerable segments of society. The erosion of trust in institutions further compounds the issue, necessitating a comprehensive approach to address the roots of corruption.

While legislative reforms, whistleblower protection, technological advancements, and civil society participation offer rays of hope, the journey towards a corruption-free society is arduous. Navigating the labyrinth requires a sustained commitment to upholding the principles of transparency, accountability, and justice. Only through collective efforts can India hope to dismantle the intricate web of corruption and pave the way for a more equitable and prosperous future.

Introduction

Child labor remains a pervasive issue in India, robbing countless children of their rightful childhoods. Despite significant progress in recent years, the prevalence of child labor continues to cast a shadow over the nation's social fabric. This article delves into the grim reality of child labor in India, examining its root causes, its implications on children's lives, and the ongoing efforts to eradicate this deeply entrenched practice.

The Faces of Child Labor

Child labor manifests in various forms, from children toiling in hazardous industries to those engaged in domestic work. The faces of child labor are diverse, reflecting the complexity of the issue. Young minds, meant for learning and growth, are often subjected to exploitation, with their innocence sacrificed at the altar of economic necessity. Understanding the diverse contexts in which child labor occurs is crucial to devising effective strategies for its eradication.

Root Causes

To address child labor effectively, it is essential to identify and comprehend its root causes. Poverty emerges as a primary factor, forcing families to rely on the income generated by their children. Lack of access to quality education exacerbates the problem, leaving children with limited opportunities for personal development. Social norms and cultural practices also contribute, normalizing child labor in certain communities. Breaking the cycle requires a multi-dimensional approach that addresses these underlying factors.

Impact on Childhood

Child labor inflicts profound and lasting damage on the lives of those involved. Deprived of education, children miss out on the chance to acquire essential skills and knowledge, perpetuating a cycle of poverty. Physical and mental health suffers as these young workers endure long hours in hazardous conditions, jeopardizing their overall well-being. The impact on their emotional and psychological development is immeasurable, leaving scars that persist into adulthood.

Legislative Framework

India has enacted various legislative measures to combat child labor, reflecting a commitment to eradicating this pervasive issue. The Child Labour (Prohibition and Regulation) Act, 1986, and subsequent amendments, aim to protect children from exploitation while outlining stringent penalties for offenders. However, effective implementation of these laws remains a challenge, with gaps persisting in enforcement and monitoring.

Educational Interventions

One of the key strategies to combat child labor is to ensure access to quality education for all children. Government initiatives such as the Sarva Shiksha Abhiyan (SSA) and the Right to Education Act aim to make education a fundamental right for every child. However, challenges such as inadequate infrastructure, teacher shortages, and socio-cultural barriers impede the success of these interventions. Strengthening the education system is crucial for breaking the cycle of child labor.

Awareness and Advocacy

Raising awareness about the consequences of child labor is pivotal in garnering support for its eradication. NGOs and grassroots organizations play a crucial role in advocacy, mobilizing communities and influencing public opinion. Campaigns that highlight the importance of education and the rights of children contribute to shifting societal attitudes towards child labor, fostering a collective commitment to its elimination.

Economic Reforms

Tackling the root cause of child labor, poverty, necessitates comprehensive economic reforms. Creating employment opportunities for adults, particularly in rural areas, can reduce the economic burden on families, diminishing the need for child labor. Implementing social welfare programs that provide financial support to vulnerable families can act as a safety net, preventing children from becoming economic assets.

Corporate Responsibility

The corporate sector plays a significant role in perpetuating or combating child labor. Adopting ethical business practices and ensuring supply chain transparency are essential steps towards eradicating child labor. Companies must adhere to responsible sourcing and production standards, conducting regular audits to identify and rectify any instances of child labor within their supply chains. Engaging in community development projects can also contribute to breaking the cycle of poverty.

Challenges in Implementation

While the legal framework and various initiatives exist, challenges persist in the effective implementation of anti-child labor measures. Limited resources, corruption, and a lack of awareness among stakeholders hinder progress. Strengthening enforcement mechanisms, enhancing coordination between government agencies and NGOs, and promoting community involvement are critical steps in overcoming these challenges.

Success Stories and Best Practices

Despite the uphill battle against child labor, there are success stories and best practices that offer hope and inspiration. Identifying and replicating these models can contribute to the formulation of more effective strategies. Communities that have successfully eradicated child labor through a combination of education, economic empowerment, and advocacy serve as beacons of change, showcasing the potential for a child labor-free future.

Conclusion

Child labor is a deeply entrenched social issue that demands collective efforts for its eradication. As India strives towards sustainable development, it is imperative to prioritize the well-being and future of its children. By addressing the root causes, strengthening the legislative framework, and fostering collaboration between government, civil society, and the corporate sector, India can pave the way for a society where every child is free to embrace the joys of a genuine childhood. The journey to eliminate child labor is arduous, but the stakes are too high

to ignore the imperative of building a nation that protects
its most precious asset – its children.

Introduction

Human trafficking stands as a pervasive and alarming issue, casting its ominous shadow across the social fabric of India. As a country grappling with various socio-economic challenges, human trafficking emerges as a significant concern, silently corroding the essence of human rights and dignity. This article delves into the intricate web of human trafficking, shedding light on its manifestations, root causes, and the ongoing efforts to combat this insidious crime.

Understanding Human Trafficking

1. Definition and Forms

Human trafficking is a grave violation of human rights, encompassing the recruitment, transportation, transfer, harboring, or receipt of individuals through force, fraud, or coercion. In India, this nefarious trade manifests in diverse forms, including sex trafficking, forced labor, child trafficking, and even organ trafficking. Each form leaves victims scarred physically, emotionally, and psychologically, perpetuating a cycle of exploitation.

2. The Vulnerable Demographics

Vulnerable groups, such as women and children, often find themselves ensnared in the clutches of traffickers. Poverty, lack of education, and social marginalization amplify their susceptibility to exploitation. Women, particularly from impoverished rural areas, are coerced into the dark alleys of sex trafficking, while children are forced into labor, robbed of their innocence and education.

Root Causes

1. Poverty and Economic Disparities

At the heart of human trafficking lies the stark reality of poverty and economic disparities. As individuals grapple with destitution, the promise of a better life becomes a tempting lure. Traffickers exploit this desperation, offering false promises of employment and prosperity, only to subject their victims to unimaginable horrors.

2. Lack of Education

A lack of education further perpetuates the vulnerability of individuals to trafficking. Without the knowledge and awareness to discern deceitful promises, victims become unwitting participants in their own exploitation. Educational initiatives, therefore, stand as a crucial component in the fight against human trafficking.

3. Gender Inequality

Gender inequality plays a pivotal role in the prevalence of human trafficking. Women and girls, often marginalized and denied equal opportunities, become easy targets for traffickers. Empowering women, ensuring equal access to education and employment, is essential to breaking the chains of exploitation.

The Faces of Exploitation

1. Sex Trafficking

Sex trafficking remains one of the most prevalent forms of exploitation, leaving countless women ensnared in a cycle of abuse. Victims are forced into prostitution, enduring physical and psychological trauma. The clandestine nature of this crime makes it challenging to rescue and rehabilitate those trapped in its clutches.

2. Forced Labor

In the dark corners of industries and households, individuals toil under the weight of forced labor. From brick kilns to domestic servitude, victims face relentless exploitation. Their stories paint a harrowing picture of lives consumed by oppression and servitude.

3. Child Trafficking

Children, robbed of their innocence, are forced into various forms of labor or pushed into the abyss of sex trafficking. The scars inflicted upon them endure, hindering their physical and emotional development. Rescuing these young souls and providing them with a chance for a normal childhood remains a critical challenge.

The Road to Redemption

1. Legal Framework and Law Enforcement

India has taken significant strides in addressing human trafficking through legislative measures. The Immoral Traffic (Prevention) Act, the Juvenile Justice (Care and Protection of Children) Act, and the Bonded Labour

System (Abolition) Act provide a legal framework for the prevention and prosecution of traffickers. However, effective enforcement and implementation remain essential.

2. Rescue and Rehabilitation

Rescue operations play a pivotal role in liberating victims from the clutches of traffickers. Collaborative efforts between law enforcement agencies, non-governmental organizations (NGOs), and community stakeholders are crucial in executing successful rescue missions. Equally important is the rehabilitation of survivors, providing them with physical, psychological, and economic support to rebuild their lives.

3. Public Awareness and Education

Raising public awareness is paramount in preventing human trafficking. Educational campaigns, both in schools and communities, can empower individuals to recognize the signs of trafficking and resist falling prey to false promises. Public awareness also fosters a sense of responsibility, encouraging citizens to report suspicious activities and contribute to the collective fight against trafficking.

Challenges and Future Prospects

1. Cross-Border Trafficking

Human trafficking often transcends national borders, making it a complex and transnational challenge. Collaborative efforts between countries, along with intelligence-sharing and coordinated law enforcement, are essential to curb cross-border trafficking networks.

2. Corruption and Impunity

Corruption within law enforcement agencies and the judiciary poses a significant hurdle in the fight against human trafficking. Eradicating corruption and ensuring accountability within these institutions are imperative to the success of anti-trafficking initiatives.

3. Empowering Vulnerable Communities

Addressing the root causes of human trafficking requires a holistic approach that empowers vulnerable communities. This involves not only economic empowerment but also initiatives that promote education, gender equality, and social inclusion. By addressing the underlying factors that make individuals susceptible to trafficking, we can create a more resilient society.

Conclusion

Human trafficking casts a long and ominous shadow over the social fabric of India, leaving in its wake shattered lives and broken dreams. However, the fight against this menace is not insurmountable. Through concerted efforts in legislation, law enforcement, public awareness, and community empowerment, we can illuminate the path toward a future free from the shadows of exploitation. It is a collective responsibility to stand against the darkness, offering hope and redemption to those ensnared in the web of human trafficking. Only then can we truly address the social issues that plague our society and pave the way for a brighter, more just future.

Introduction

In recent years, the discourse surrounding LGBTQ+ rights in India has undergone a transformative shift, with both societal attitudes and legal frameworks evolving. While there has been considerable progress, challenges persist, reflecting a complex interplay of cultural, legal, and societal factors. This article delves into the current status of LGBTQ+ rights in India, examining the milestones achieved and the ongoing struggle for acceptance.

Historical Context

To understand the contemporary LGBTQ+ rights movement in India, it is crucial to delve into its historical context. The colonial-era Section 377 of the Indian Penal Code criminalized same-sex relationships, casting a long shadow on the LGBTQ+ community for decades. The watershed moment came in 2018 when the Supreme Court of India decriminalized consensual same-sex relationships, marking a significant victory for the LGBTQ+ community.

Legal Milestones

Post the decriminalization of homosexuality, the legal landscape in India has witnessed additional milestones. The Transgender Persons (Protection of Rights) Act, 2019 aimed to recognize and safeguard the rights of transgender individuals, offering legal recognition and protection against discrimination. However, the legislation faced criticism for its perceived inadequacies and lack of comprehensive protection.

Challenges in Legal Implementation

Despite the progressive legal changes, the implementation of LGBTQ+ rights remains a challenge. The transgender community, in particular, faces hurdles in obtaining legal recognition and benefits. Discrimination, both subtle and overt, persists, highlighting the need for robust mechanisms to ensure the effective enforcement of existing laws.

Societal Attitudes and Acceptance

While legal changes provide a solid foundation, societal attitudes play a pivotal role in the true acceptance of LGBTQ+ individuals. India's diverse cultural tapestry encompasses a range of attitudes towards non-normative sexual orientations and gender identities. Urban areas may exhibit greater acceptance, but rural regions often grapple with deeply ingrained societal norms.

Media Representation

Media plays a crucial role in shaping public opinion, and its portrayal of LGBTQ+ individuals has a profound impact on societal attitudes. In recent years, there has been a noticeable shift in media representation, with films and television shows featuring LGBTQ+ characters in more nuanced and positive roles. This, in turn, contributes to increased visibility and understanding.

Education and Awareness

Addressing social issues necessitates a robust educational framework that fosters inclusivity and awareness. Incorporating LGBTQ+ issues into school curricula can pave the way for a more accepting society. While some progress has been made, a comprehensive and standardized approach to LGBTQ+ education is yet to be fully realized.

Healthcare Disparities

The LGBTQ+ community faces unique healthcare challenges, including limited access to affirmative care and the prevalence of stigma within the healthcare system. Culturally competent healthcare practices, coupled with awareness campaigns, are crucial in bridging these gaps and ensuring that LGBTQ+ individuals receive the care they need without fear of discrimination.

Corporate Inclusivity

The corporate sector is increasingly recognizing the importance of inclusivity in the workplace. Many organizations have implemented policies and initiatives to create a more LGBTQ+-friendly environment. However, challenges such as workplace discrimination and the lack of comprehensive anti-discrimination laws pose obstacles to achieving full workplace equality.

Religious Perspectives

India's diverse religious landscape adds another layer to the discussion on LGBTQ+ rights. While some religious groups have embraced inclusivity, others maintain conservative views, contributing to a complex interplay between faith and LGBTQ+ acceptance. Dialogues between LGBTQ+ advocates and religious leaders are crucial to fostering understanding and dispelling misconceptions.

Intersectionality

The LGBTQ+ community is not a monolith, and issues of intersectionality further complicate the struggle for rights and acceptance. Individuals belonging to marginalized communities within the LGBTQ+ spectrum, such as queer people of color and disabled LGBTQ+ individuals, face compounded challenges. Recognizing and addressing these intersecting identities is essential for a truly inclusive movement.

Ongoing Advocacy Efforts

Despite the progress made, the fight for LGBTQ+ rights in India is far from over. Advocacy groups continue to work towards comprehensive legal protections, increased awareness, and societal acceptance. Grassroots movements, pride events, and online activism play a crucial role in amplifying the voices of the LGBTQ+ community and allies. *Pride events* are celebratory gatherings, parades, and activities organized by the LGBTQ+ community and its allies to promote visibility, equality, and acceptance, typically held during significant occasions.

Global Perspectives

The LGBTQ+ rights movement in India is interconnected with global efforts for equality. Lessons learned from international experiences, both successes and setbacks, can inform strategies for advancing LGBTQ+ rights in the Indian context. Collaborative efforts with global organizations can provide valuable resources and support for local advocacy.

Conclusion

The journey towards LGBTQ+ acceptance in India is marked by significant strides and persistent challenges. Legal victories, changing societal attitudes, and ongoing advocacy efforts collectively shape the narrative of progress. However, the path forward requires a comprehensive approach that addresses legal gaps, societal prejudices, and intersectional challenges. As India grapples with these complexities, the ongoing struggle for LGBTQ+ rights remains a testament to the resilience and determination of a community seeking nothing more than the right to live authentically and without fear of discrimination.

Introduction

Urbanization is an inevitable global phenomenon, and India, with its burgeoning population and rapid economic growth, is no exception. As the country witnesses the relentless expansion of its urban areas, the challenges associated with this urbanization are becoming increasingly pronounced. The concrete jungle, once hailed as a symbol of progress, now grapples with a myriad of issues that affect the well-being of its inhabitants. This article delves into the challenges posed by rapid urbanization in India and explores potential urban planning solutions to address these issues.

Population Explosion and Infrastructure Strain

One of the primary challenges of urbanization in India is the unprecedented population explosion. As rural migrants flock to cities in search of better opportunities, the urban landscape is grappling with a strain on its infrastructure. Overcrowded public transport, inadequate sanitation facilities, and stretched healthcare services are symptomatic of this strain. The rapid influx of people often outpaces the ability of urban planners to create sustainable and efficient infrastructure, resulting in a domino effect on the quality of life in these urban areas.

Domino effect is a chain reaction where a single event or occurrence triggers a sequence of similar events, each causing the next one in line to happen. The term is often used to describe a cumulative and interconnected series of events, where the impact of the initial incident propagates through a system, influencing and leading to subsequent events.

Lack of Affordable Housing

The dream of a better life often lures individuals to urban centers, but the reality they encounter is starkly different. A significant challenge arising from urbanization is the acute shortage of affordable housing. Skyrocketing real estate prices and limited government initiatives to address this issue force many to live in informal settlements or slums. This not only compromises the safety and well-being of residents but also creates a stark divide between the haves and have-nots in the urban landscape.

Environmental Degradation

The unchecked expansion of urban areas often comes at a steep environmental cost. Rapid deforestation, air and water pollution, and the *heat island effect* (urban areas experiencing higher temperatures than surrounding rural areas due to human activities like construction and reduced green spaces, impacting local climates and energy consumption) are some of the consequences of this phenomenon. Urbanization accelerates the depletion of natural resources, disrupts ecosystems, and contributes to climate change. Striking a balance between development and environmental sustainability is a critical challenge that urban planners must grapple with to ensure a healthier and sustainable future.

Traffic Congestion and Air Quality

As urban areas swell with population, so does the number of vehicles on the roads. Traffic congestion has become synonymous with urban living in India, leading to increased commuting times, productivity losses, and heightened levels of stress. Moreover, the surge in vehicular traffic contributes significantly to air pollution. Poor air quality, characterized by high levels of pollutants, poses severe health risks to the urban population. Addressing traffic congestion and improving air quality are imperative for creating livable and healthy urban environments.

Water Scarcity and Wastewater Management

The burgeoning population in urban areas places immense pressure on water resources. The demand for water for domestic, industrial, and agricultural purposes often exceeds the available supply. Additionally, improper wastewater management further compounds the problem. Untreated sewage and industrial effluents contaminate water bodies, leading to waterborne diseases and environmental degradation. Urban planning must prioritize sustainable water management practices, including recycling and efficient distribution, to mitigate the impacts of water scarcity.

Social Inequality and Gentrification

Gentrification is the process of urban renewal where wealthier individuals or groups invest in and renovate deteriorating neighborhoods, leading to increased property values, improved infrastructure, and cultural changes. While it often enhances the urban landscape, gentrification can also displace long-term residents, causing social and economic challenges.

Urbanization tends to exacerbate existing social inequalities and, in some cases, gives rise to new forms of discrimination. Gentrification, driven by the influx of affluent individuals into once-ignored neighborhoods, often displaces the original residents. This process can lead to the erosion of local cultures and the alienation of marginalized communities. Urban planning solutions must prioritize inclusive development, ensuring that the benefits of urbanization are distributed equitably among all sections of the society.

Inadequate Healthcare and Educational Facilities

The strain on urban infrastructure is particularly evident in the inadequacy of healthcare and educational facilities. Rapid population growth often outpaces the expansion of essential services, leaving a significant portion of the urban population without access to quality healthcare and education. This not only hampers individual well-being but also limits the overall development potential of urban areas. Strategic urban planning should focus on the equitable distribution of healthcare and educational resources to address this critical challenge.

Employment Disparities and Informal Sector

Informal sector involves unregulated economic activities, often involving self-employment and small enterprises, lacking formal contracts and government oversight, leading to challenges in job security and access to benefits for workers.

While urbanization promises economic opportunities, the reality for many is the prevalence of employment disparities and the dominance of the informal sector. A large segment of the urban population engages in informal, low-paying jobs with minimal job security. This perpetuates poverty and economic vulnerability, hindering the overall socio-economic development of urban areas.

Urban planning solutions should emphasize the creation of sustainable and inclusive economic opportunities to uplift the urban workforce.

Smart Urban Planning Solutions

Addressing the challenges posed by rapid urbanization requires innovative and sustainable urban planning solutions. Here are some key strategies:

Integrated Urban Planning: Adopting a holistic approach to urban planning that considers the interplay of infrastructure, environment, and social factors is crucial. Integrated urban planning helps create resilient and sustainable urban ecosystems.

Affordable Housing Initiatives: Governments and urban planners should prioritize affordable housing initiatives to bridge the gap between demand and supply. Incentives for developers, public-private partnerships, and innovative housing models can contribute to this endeavor.

Green Infrastructure: Integrating green spaces, parks, and sustainable landscaping into urban planning helps mitigate the environmental impact of urbanization. Green infrastructure not only enhances the quality of life but also contributes to ecological balance.

Public Transportation and Traffic Management: Investing in efficient public transportation systems and implementing intelligent traffic management solutions can alleviate congestion and improve air quality. Promoting alternative modes of transport, such as cycling and walking, can also reduce reliance on private vehicles.

Water Conservation and Management: Implementing water conservation measures, promoting rainwater harvesting, and investing in efficient wastewater treatment plants are essential for addressing water scarcity. Sustainable water management practices can ensure a steady and equitable supply of water.

Inclusive Development Policies: Urban planning should prioritize inclusive development policies that address social inequalities. This includes measures to prevent gentrification, promote community engagement, and ensure equal access to basic amenities and services.

Health and Education Infrastructure: Investing in healthcare and education infrastructure is crucial for the well-being and development of urban populations. Building more hospitals, schools, and vocational training centers can cater to the growing needs of urban residents.

Promotion of Sustainable Industries: Encouraging the growth of sustainable industries and providing support for small and medium enterprises can diversify the urban economy. This, in turn, reduces dependence on the informal sector and creates more stable employment opportunities.

Conclusion

As India continues its journey towards becoming a global economic powerhouse, the challenges of rapid urbanization cannot be ignored. The concrete jungle must transform into a sustainable and inclusive habitat that fosters the well-being of its residents. Urban planning solutions that prioritize environmental sustainability, social equity, and economic inclusivity are imperative to address the urbanization blues and pave the way for a brighter and more sustainable urban future in India. By learning from past mistakes and embracing innovative approaches, urban areas can evolve into vibrant hubs of progress without compromising the welfare of their inhabitants.

Introduction

India, a land of diversity, rich cultural tapestry, and historical complexities, stands at the crossroads of progress and challenges. The preceding chapters of this book have meticulously unraveled the myriad social issues that persist in the country. As we delve into the future prospects, it is imperative to explore the potential for a more inclusive and equitable India. In this chapter, we will analyze ongoing efforts and emerging trends that signify a collective march towards a brighter, more integrated society.

Technological Innovations

The rapid pace of technological advancements presents a double-edged sword in the context of social issues. On one hand, it has the potential to exacerbate existing inequalities, but on the other, it offers innovative solutions to age-old problems. With the advent of digital platforms, access to information and services is no longer a privilege but a necessity. Initiatives such as digital literacy programs and online healthcare consultations are gradually bridging the urban-rural divide, bringing essential services to the fingertips of those who need them the most.

However, it is crucial to ensure that these technological solutions are inclusive and reach marginalized communities. The government, NGOs, and private enterprises must collaborate to harness the full potential of technology in addressing social disparities.

Economic Reforms

Economic policies play a pivotal role in shaping the socio-economic landscape of a nation. India's tryst with economic reforms has been a journey of highs and lows. The emphasis on inclusive growth is gaining prominence, with targeted schemes focusing on poverty alleviation, job creation, and skill development. The government's flagship programs like 'Make in India' and 'Skill India' aim to empower the marginalized by providing them with opportunities to participate in the country's economic growth.

However, it is imperative to monitor the implementation of these policies to ensure that the benefits trickle down to the grassroots level. Transparency and accountability in governance become crucial factors in building a more inclusive economy.

Strengthening Educational Ecosystems

Education is a powerful tool for social transformation. In the pursuit of an inclusive India, addressing educational inequities becomes paramount. Initiatives such as the Right to Education Act have laid the foundation for universal access to education. However, the quality of education, especially in rural areas, remains a challenge.

To build an inclusive India, it is essential to revamp the educational infrastructure, focus on teacher training, and introduce curriculum reforms that promote diversity and inclusivity. Collaboration between the government, NGOs, and local communities can play a pivotal role in creating an educational ecosystem that nurtures the potential of every child.

Gender Sensitization

Chapter 8 delves into the complexities of gender inequality, emphasizing the need for breaking societal chains that confine individuals based on their gender. The future prospects of building an inclusive India heavily depend on dismantling these stereotypes and fostering an environment where every individual, irrespective of gender, has equal opportunities and rights.

Government initiatives like 'Beti Bachao, Beti Padhao' and the push for increased representation of women in various sectors are steps in the right direction. However, a sustained effort is required to challenge deep-rooted patriarchal norms and create an inclusive society where individuals are judged on their capabilities rather than their gender.

Social Activism and Grassroots Movements

As explored in Chapter 3, NGOs and grassroots movements are the unsung heroes in the fight against social issues. The future of an inclusive India relies heavily on the continued efforts of these catalysts for change. These organizations bridge the gap between policy formulations and on-ground realities, advocating for the rights of the marginalized and holding authorities accountable.

To build an inclusive India, it is essential to empower and support these organizations. Strengthening their capacities, ensuring financial sustainability, and acknowledging their role as partners in social change are crucial steps towards a more equitable society.

Environmental Sustainability

Chapter 12 discusses the challenges of environmental stewardship in the face of rapid urbanization and industrialization. Building an inclusive India necessitates a sustainable approach that balances economic growth with environmental conservation. The emergence of green technologies, renewable energy sources, and eco-friendly practices can pave the way for a harmonious coexistence between development and nature.

Government policies promoting sustainable practices, corporate responsibility towards the environment, and public awareness campaigns can collectively contribute to creating a future where growth does not come at the expense of the planet.

Inclusive Healthcare

Access to healthcare is a fundamental right, yet millions in India face barriers in obtaining basic medical services. Chapter 11 highlights the challenges in healthcare access, and the future prospects of an inclusive India hinge on addressing these issues. Strengthening the healthcare infrastructure, ensuring affordable and accessible services, and promoting preventive healthcare are essential steps in this direction.

Public-private partnerships, community health initiatives, and technological innovations can play a significant role in building a healthcare system that caters to the diverse needs of the population, leaving no one behind.

Social Harmony

Chapters 10 and 16 delve into the challenges posed by religious intolerance and the struggles faced by the LGBTQ+ community. Building an inclusive India requires fostering social harmony, where diversity is not just tolerated but celebrated. Educational curricula promoting cultural understanding, media campaigns against discrimination, and stringent legal measures to protect the rights of marginalized communities are vital components of this journey.

The youth, as agents of change (Chapter 5), can play a crucial role in fostering tolerance and acceptance. Educational institutions and community organizations must actively engage in dialogue and awareness programs to break down prejudices and stereotypes.

Urbanization with a Human Touch

As highlighted in Chapter 17, urbanization brings its own set of challenges, including slums, congestion, and unequal distribution of resources. The future of urban India lies in smart, inclusive urbanization that prioritizes the well-being of its residents. Sustainable urban planning, affordable housing, and inclusive infrastructure development can transform cities into hubs of opportunity rather than pockets of disparity.

Navigating the Labyrinth of Corruption

Chapter 13 explores the pervasive issue of corruption, a stumbling block in the path to an inclusive India. Transparent governance, stringent anti-corruption measures, and an empowered judiciary are essential in curbing corruption. Additionally, creating a culture of ethical conduct and accountability within institutions and the public at large is crucial for building a society where resources are allocated fairly and justly.

Charting Paths to a Better Tomorrow

In the concluding chapter, we reflect on the collective responsibility of individuals, communities, and institutions in charting paths to a better tomorrow. The chapters preceding this one have painted a comprehensive picture of the social issues plaguing India, but they have also illuminated the potential for positive change.

Building an inclusive India requires collaboration between the government, NGOs, the private sector, and the citizens themselves. It demands a commitment to justice, equality, and sustainable development. As we envision a future where every individual, regardless of their background, enjoys the fruits of progress, it is crucial to remember that the journey towards inclusivity is ongoing.

In conclusion, the future prospects of building an inclusive India are promising but contingent on sustained efforts, policy reforms, and societal transformations. The chapters in this book collectively serve as a guidebook for understanding, confronting, and ultimately overcoming the social issues that hinder the realization of a truly inclusive and equitable nation.

As we draw the final curtains on this comprehensive exploration of social issues in India, it becomes evident that the journey towards a better tomorrow is both challenging and promising. The preceding chapters have delved deep into the various facets of India's social landscape, dissecting problems, and seeking solutions. Now, in this concluding chapter, we reflect on the collective efforts, challenges faced, and potential solutions discussed across the spectrum of issues. We also propose a vision for a socially just and inclusive India that embraces diversity, equality, and progress.

Reflecting on Collective Efforts

The collective efforts made by individuals, communities, NGOs, the government, and various stakeholders have been instrumental in addressing social issues in India. Grassroots movements, as highlighted in Chapter 3, have been the bedrock of change, challenging the status quo and amplifying the voices of the marginalized. Government policies, discussed in Chapter 2, have played a crucial role in shaping the social landscape, though not without challenges and criticisms. NGOs have served as catalysts for change, filling gaps where governmental interventions fall short.

Youth activism, explored in Chapter 5, emerged as a powerful force driving change. The passion, energy, and idealism of the youth have led to significant movements, demanding accountability and justice. Media, as discussed in Chapter 4, has been both a mirror and a shaper of social narratives, influencing public opinion and driving conversations on crucial issues. The collaborative efforts across these sectors have laid the groundwork for progress.

Challenges Faced Along the Way

However, the journey has not been without hurdles. Poverty, educational inequities, gender inequality, the caste system, religious intolerance, healthcare disparities, environmental concerns, corruption, child labor, human trafficking, LGBTQ+ rights, and urbanization challenges – each issue presented its unique set of obstacles. Tackling these problems requires a multifaceted approach, acknowledging the interconnectedness of social issues.

Overcoming deeply ingrained societal norms and biases, as seen in the struggles against gender inequality and the caste system, requires not just legal reforms but a cultural shift. The fight against poverty and educational inequities demands sustained efforts in resource allocation and systemic changes. Balancing economic growth with environmental sustainability is a tightrope walk that necessitates innovative policies and conscientious decision-making.

Potential Solutions Explored

Amidst the challenges, the potential solutions explored in each chapter offer rays of hope. Grassroots movements have showcased the power of community-driven initiatives in bringing about change. Government policies, when well-implemented and inclusive, can be transformative. NGOs continue to bridge gaps, providing support and advocacy where it is most needed.

The role of media in shaping narratives and influencing public opinion should not be underestimated. Responsible journalism and media literacy can contribute significantly to dispelling stereotypes and fostering understanding. Youth activism, with its vigor and passion, can continue to be a driving force, pushing the boundaries of what is deemed possible.

A Vision for a Socially Just and Inclusive India

As we chart paths to a better tomorrow, envisioning a socially just and inclusive India becomes paramount. This vision necessitates collaborative efforts, with the government, civil society, and the private sector working hand in hand. It begins with acknowledging the interconnectedness of social issues and adopting an intersectional approach in policymaking.

1. Education as the Cornerstone

A socially just India must prioritize education as the cornerstone of progress. Bridging educational inequities and ensuring quality education for all, irrespective of socio-economic background, is pivotal. This includes addressing issues such as unequal access to educational resources, outdated curriculum, and the digital divide.

2. Economic Empowerment

Eradicating poverty requires not just charity but economic empowerment. Creating sustainable livelihoods, promoting entrepreneurship, and ensuring fair wages are key components. Empowering marginalized communities through skill development and employment opportunities can break the cycle of poverty.

3. Gender Equality in all Spheres

A socially just India must be one where gender equality is not just a slogan but a lived reality. This involves dismantling patriarchal structures, ensuring equal opportunities in education and employment, and fostering an environment where every individual, regardless of gender, can thrive.

4. Environmental Sustainability

Balancing economic growth with environmental stewardship is a delicate dance. A sustainable future involves investing in renewable energy, promoting eco-friendly practices, and preserving biodiversity. It requires a shift towards conscious consumption and responsible urbanization.

5. Inclusive Policies

Inclusivity should be embedded in every policy decision. This includes affirmative action to address historical injustices, ensuring representation of diverse voices in decision-making bodies, and actively dismantling discriminatory practices in all spheres of life.

6. Healthcare Access for All

Healthcare should be a universal right, not a privilege. Strengthening healthcare infrastructure, ensuring affordable and accessible medical services, and prioritizing preventive healthcare can contribute to a healthier and more resilient society.

7. Nurturing Social Harmony

Fostering religious tolerance, promoting dialogue, and celebrating diversity are essential for social harmony. It involves challenging divisive narratives and building bridges of understanding between communities.

8. Eradicating Social Evils

Rooting out social evils like corruption, child labor, and human trafficking requires stringent legal measures, but also societal awareness and active participation. It involves creating a culture where exploitation is condemned, and the rights of every individual are protected.

9. LGBTQ+ Inclusivity

A socially just India is one that embraces and celebrates its LGBTQ+ community. It involves legal reforms, awareness campaigns, and creating safe spaces where individuals can express their identities without fear of discrimination.

10. Sustainable Urbanization

As India urbanizes, it must do so sustainably. This includes planning cities with a focus on green spaces, efficient public transportation, and affordable housing. It involves addressing the challenges of rapid urbanization while preserving the cultural fabric of communities.

The Path Forward

Realizing this vision requires commitment, perseverance, and a collective will to confront the complex web of social issues. It demands continuous dialogue, learning from both successes and failures, and adapting strategies based on evolving realities.

It's crucial to recognize that change is a gradual process, and the transformation envisioned might not happen overnight. However, with sustained efforts, the seeds planted today can blossom into a more just and inclusive India tomorrow.

In conclusion, as we navigate the intricate tapestry of social issues in India, let us not forget that the power to shape the future lies in our collective hands. Each chapter of this book has been a step towards understanding and addressing the challenges that our society faces. The concluding chapter serves as a call to action, urging us to come together, transcend boundaries, and forge a path to a better tomorrow – a tomorrow where every individual, regardless of their background, has an equal opportunity to thrive and contribute to the vibrant tapestry of our nation. The journey towards a socially just and inclusive India is ongoing, and the chapters written today will define the narrative of our shared tomorrow.

"Addressing Social Issues in India" offers a comprehensive exploration of the myriad challenges shaping the socio-cultural fabric of the nation. The book delves into the diverse landscape of social issues, beginning with an insightful overview in the first chapter. Subsequent chapters meticulously dissect the influence of government policies, the pivotal role played by NGOs and grassroots movements, and the impact of media on public perceptions. The narrative extends to encompass the dynamic contributions of youth activism and the persistent struggles against poverty, educational inequities, gender inequality, and the historical legacy of the caste system.

The book investigates religious harmony, healthcare challenges, environmental stewardship, corruption, child labor, human trafficking, LGBTQ+ rights, and the repercussions of rapid urbanization. The concluding chapters envision a more inclusive future, synthesizing collective efforts and proposing a roadmap for a socially just and equitable India. "Addressing Social Issues in India" serves as an indispensable resource for scholars, policymakers, and activists committed to fostering positive change in the country.

ABOUT THE AUTHOR

Mr. C. P. Kumar is a retired Scientist 'G' from National Institute of Hydrology, Roorkee, Uttarakhand, India. He is also a Reiki Healer and Chakra Balancing practitioner (with pendulum dowsing) and offers Emotional Freedom Technique (EFT) to help individuals with emotional issues. Mr. Kumar has authored many books on technical, spiritual, and social topics.

For further details, you may visit his webpage
https://www.angelfire.com/nh/cpkumar/virgo.html